Table of Contents

Rourke Educational Media

rourkeeducationalmedia.com

Can you find these words?

cares

listens

shares

together

What Friends Do

Friends are kind to each other.

A friend helps.

"We can do it together!"

A friend **shares.**

"You can read my book."

A friend **listens**.
"Why are you sad?"

A friend **cares.**

"I'm sorry you are hurt."

A friend takes turns.

"You can play next!"
Are you a friend?

Did you find these words?

A friend **cares.**

A friend **listens.**

A friend **shares.**

"We can do it **together!**"

Photo Glossary

cares (kairs): A person cares when they feel interest or concern.

listens (LIS-uhns): A person listens when they give attention to words or sounds.

shares (shairs): A person shares when they give something to someone else.

together (tuh-geTH-ur): Together means to do something with another person.

Index

About the Author

Charlotte Hunter writes books about everything from friendship to fruit. When she's not writing, she enjoys going for long walks with her dog, Penny.

www.rourkeeducationalmedia.com

PHOTO CREDITS: Cover ©Viorika, © kirin_photo, Page 3 ©By Golden Pixels LLC, Page 2,4-5,14,15 ©By ZouZou, Page 2,6-7,14,15 ©andresr, Page 2,8-9,14,15 ©szefei, Page 2,10-11,14,15 ©By MNStudio, Page 12-13 ©gilaxia

Edited by: Keli Sipperley
Cover design by: Kathy Walsh
Interior design by: Rhea Magaro-Wallace

Library of Congress PCN Data
What Friends Do / Charlotte Hunter
(Let's Learn)
ISBN (hard cover)(alk. paper) 978-1-64156-167-9
ISBN (soft cover) 978-1-64156-223-2
ISBN (e-Book) 978-1-64156-277-5
Library of Congress Control Number:2017957778

Printed in the United States of America, North Mankato, Minnesota